"mPWR¹⁰ is akin to an essential checklist for life – a 10 minute investment in building a framework for positive action which can really contribute to daily success. I'm using it with my team with great results."

**– Brian Lortie, Senior Vice-President,
Branded Pharmaceuticals,
Endo Pharmaceuticals**

"This 10 minutes a day of mental training helped me achieve my goal of making the major leagues. mPWR¹⁰ is a 'game changer' that I only wish I had in college or earlier in my career."

– Mike Costanzo, Professional Baseball Player

"The mPWR¹⁰ process outlined in ON TRACK enabled me to crystallize and make significant progress toward my goals. And by starting my day off with mPWR¹⁰, I'm overall more prepared for the opportunities, challenges and adversities that inevitably come my way. For players, mPWR¹⁰ gives them a mental framework enabling them to perform more consistently at their best."

**– Mike Murphy, Men's Head Lacrosse Coach,
University of Pennsylvania**

"Using the techniques you'll find in ON TRACK, our company has experienced phenomenal growth. We went from a start-up company doing about $1M in revenue to doing $10M in revenue within a year! This is the most intelligently designed system to gain quick results that I have utilized in my 20 years of business."

**– George Griffith, Managing Partner and
Chief Strategy Officer, ConneXion360**

"The mPWR¹⁰ 10-minute-a-day routine helps me set purpose for my day. It helps me direct my thoughts in a positive way and be the best I can be each day."

**– Peter Hissey, Portland Sea Dogs,
AA affiliate of the Boston Red Sox**

*"ON TRACK is phenomenal. The mPWR[10] tool is easy
and powerful, and it does only take 10 minutes. I highly
recommend it for EVERYONE. Among its many benefits:
I stay more focused on important things, with a more positive
attitude, and less "overwhelmed" from all the different tugs
at my time."*

**– Jeffrie Story, Author of Straight to Great:
The Sale's Manager Field Guide**

*"I practice diligently and benefit from the mPWR[10] habits
both personally and professionally. For me, it has been a life-
changing experience, which helped me to do more with less
while being excited each day about what lies ahead in life.
I highly recommend mPWR[10] to any executives who are trying
to balance all the demands in life while achieving maximum
performance. Try it and you will find yourself passionate about
people, work and more importantly life!"*

**– James Huang, Managing Partner,
KPCP Venture Capital**

*"Whether you want to succeed on the basketball court, in
sales, business or in life overall, it all starts with a winning
mindset. If you apply the techniques in ON TRACK, you'll
change the way you think and I'm confident you'll enhance
your results and remain resilient in the face of the obstacles
along the way."*

**– Steve Donahue, Head Men's Basketball Coach,
Boston College**

*"mPWR[10] works! I'm amazed at the immediate tangible
results. My confidence has soared and my positive energy
has resulted in numerous new fruitful business opportunities.
And despite the difficult retail economy, each of my team's
departments is exceeding their goals as well."*

**– Kim Gallia, General Sales Manager,
Ardmore Toyota, Ardmore, PA**

"The rewards you receive from this small investment of time are incredible! I would recommend ON TRACK to anyone who wants to get more out of life and feel great along the way."

**– Robert Sterba, President,
RCS Fitness Systems**

"mPWR[10] enables my coaching clients to use a structured process to reinforce proven practices from the field of Positive & Peak Performance Psychology. My clients are amazed at the immediate tangible results they achieve by spending just minutes a day."

**– Paula Shoup, ACC, Executive and
Team Coach at www.myinternalGPS.com**

"mPWR[10] helped me get back on track and reach high level goals as I have in the past. First, it allows you to get connected with your meaningful goals and aspirations and then helps you reach them by moving past internal and external obstacles."

**– Mary Hall, Executive Account Manager,
Hallmark Residential**

"ON TRACK provides a highly effective and tangible tool that in just minutes a day allows you to easily translate your personal & professional goals into measurable execution."

**– Gerald Mosely, Former Global
General Manager, Baxter Healthcare
and Sales Vice President, GlaxoSmithKline**

"As a business owner and coach, mPWR[10] is a great asset to me personally and to use with my clients. The 10-minute daily practice keeps us resilient and focused on our most important goals."

**– Debra Exner, PCC, CPCC, Vice President
National Speakers Association Arizona**

ON TRACK:

More Success,
Less Stress
In 10 Minutes a Day

Michelle Chung
Nancy Donahue

www.mpwr10.com

To Danny

Your memory inspires us to live on track.
Your spirit continues to guide us.

Contents

Background and *mPWR¹⁰* Overview

Stress has been declared as the "health epidemic of the 21st century" by the World Health Organization and is costing American businesses up to $300 billion a year in lost productivity. This is not surprising given the economic uncertainties, 24/7 demanding lifestyles and continual changes and challenges. However, we don't have to let these things control us and lead us to feel like we're just surviving each day. The good news is that human beings are intrinsically hardwired to set and achieve goals, to grow and thrive. The question is how best to focus our energy and maximize results. Imagine that a small amount of time invested in yourself each day could enable you to take control and create what you want in all areas of your life. *mPWR¹⁰* is a revolutionary 10-minute-a-day structured process that empowers you to stay on track, perform at your best on a daily basis regardless of challenges and circumstances, and realize meaningful goals while experiencing less stress.

Several years ago while working together in the pharmaceutical industry, we were exposed to cutting-edge scientific studies demonstrating that by implementing specific habits you can replicate your best performance on a routine basis. Reflecting back on our many years of corporate management experience, we realized we had seen this science at work first hand among the most successful individuals and effective leaders. The reliability and consistency of their performance was driven by their ability to stay focused, optimistic and solution-oriented despite the pressure.

This inspired us to develop a way for people to easily and effectively use these principles to thrive, take their results to a higher level and sustain them. So, we extensively researched, analyzed and synthesized the Peak Performance, Positive Psychology and Leadership literature and arrived at the six *mPWR[10]* habits that were consistently proven to be essential for success.

Of course, to sustain meaningful changes, it's not enough just to know what to do. Taking action is the key. Probably, like us, you've had the experience of listening to a motivational speaker or reading personal growth or leadership books and felt extremely inspired and anticipated implementing the recommendations. However, after the positive emotion has waned several days later, what tends to happen? Most people will say, "Not much," "I get busy and fall back to my old habits," or "I forget what I am supposed to do."

So here you'll learn a practical and proven technique to easily apply each of the *mPWR[10]* habits. And you'll have the opportunity to practice these techniques using the *mPWR[10]* process. The *mPWR[10]* process is very effective for two reasons. First, it's a structured framework that enables you to practice all six of these proven habits in just 10 minutes. What could be easier than that? Second, writing and recording acts as a filter for the brain and gives importance to what you're actively focusing on, thus diminishing any distractions.

Uniquely, by spending just 10 minutes a day implementing these techniques, you are taking personal accountability for how you want to perform and will immediately observe tangible benefits.

Many now look forward to completing *mPWR¹⁰* and it has become the most important 10 minutes of their day because it easily sets them up for success. They are in control rather than having circumstances controlling them and they stay positive, confident and focused on meaningful priorities. We hope you also embrace this opportunity to routinely be at your best and stay on track to achieve more personal success in all areas of your life.

*"I've had an amazing experience going through mPWR¹⁰! It has truly changed my life, perspective and results. In every role that I play – mother, wife, daughter, colleague, sales professional, I seek success. mPWR¹⁰ helps you learn effective habits that make success an ease. It helps you focus on and achieve what you want out of life with a smile on your face." – **Carli F.**

Compelling Evidence Supporting an Empowered Mindset

houghts are not invisible, insignificant things. Frequent dominant thoughts, especially those that are emotionally charged, have significant power. This concept is the cornerstone of *mPWR[10]*. Our thoughts are powerful because they drive our emotions. Emotions impact the actions we take – and the results we achieve. Consider, for example, if you are thinking negatively and/or focusing on things outside of your control such as the poor economy or risk of layoffs. Naturally, emotions such as worry, fear and anxiety will be triggered, which are distracting and compromise your results. On the other hand, we are empowered to create what we want in our lives by maintaining positive thoughts and emotions which ensure that we communicate effectively and perform at peak levels.

> *We become what we think about most of the time.*
>
> **Earl Nightingale**

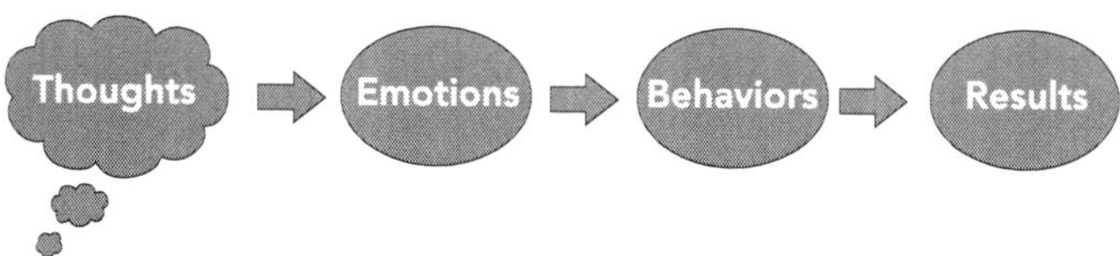

Many people are unaware of how powerful their mindsets are. Rather than focusing on what they truly want, their focus and self-talk is on what they don't want. They unwittingly create the same old behavior patterns which lead to the unwanted, however familiar, results and outcomes. For example, people want to be healthy and fit but say, "I hate being overweight." They want to be successful in their careers but are thinking about all the obstacles in their way. Or they want a loving committed relationship but are focused on being single and lonely. The choice is yours.

You are empowered to change your life for the better by shifting your thoughts and words and keeping them focused on what you want to achieve. To determine precisely where your focus is, pay attention to how you feel. When your thoughts are focused on what you want, you feel empowered. When your thoughts are focused on what you do not want, you feel negative emotions.

Joseph Dowling, a specialist in Peak Performance Psychology, often works with athletes, corporate professionals and artists. He emphasizes to his clients the extraordinary value of a empowered mindset in enhancing performance. He often begins by teaching his clients the important difference between the conscious and the subconscious mind. The conscious mind is the part of the mind that analyzes, organizes things and gets you through your day by structuring what you need to do and how to do it. However, it's also the part of your mind that is negative and critical. It's the worrying, the ruminating, the clatter, chatter, and the 'what if' part of your mind. It's analogist to a one-channel television with programs that illuminate only the negative, the problems, the failure, doom and gloom.

The good news, Dowling teaches, is that the subconscious mind is like a satellite television with seemingly endless channels that magnify positivity, possibilities, creativity, solutions and achieving goals. When you are tapping into the subconscious, it takes you from feeling distracted and overwhelmed to focused and in control. This is your natural state, your peak performance zone, and where your very best self lives. It is always there and you can access it seamlessly and perform at optimal levels by utilizing the *mPWR*[10] habits. On a daily basis, you can be creative, solution-oriented and resilient, and stay on track to achieve what you want in your personal and professional life.

Not surprisingly, a growing body of compelling evidence supports the multiple interrelated benefits of a positive mindset. Fredrickson and Joiner (2002) studied the ways that a positive versus negative mindset affects a person's ability to cope with challenges. They found that those with more negative emotions were narrow-minded and had low coping scores when dealing with problems. Whereas those with positive mindsets faced troubles with an open mind, allowing them to see a wide range of possibilities and find solutions.

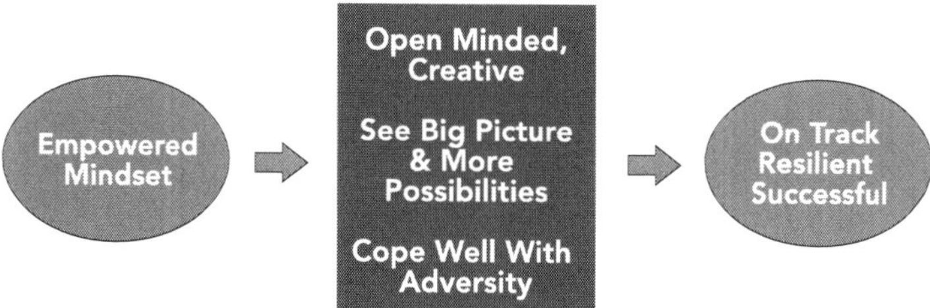

You are empowered to choose your focus and utilize your energy to create positive solutions rather than be taken over by the problem. Remember, it isn't the situation but how we respond to it that causes our positive or negative emotions.

Have you ever noticed how individuals and teams with a positive mindset act during times of challenge? They act empowered. They look for the good or what is working well in the situation. They collaborate, open their minds to possibilities and generate solutions to move forward productively. This approach enables them to be successful.

Research has demonstrated that a positive mindset enhances resilience (Fredrickson, Tugade, Waugh, Larkin, 2003), protects against developing disability and other physical declines of aging, and even enhances longevity (Ostir, Markides, Black, Goodwin, 2000).

> *… positivity can transform individuals for the better, making them healthier, more socially integrated, knowledgeable, effective, and resilient.*
> **Barbara Fredrickson and Marcial Losada, 2005**

The correlation between a positive mindset and success is also born out in studies with employees in the business setting. Staw, Sutton & Pelled (1994) measured emotions in 272 employees and then followed their job performance for the next 18 months. Employees with positive emotions received more favorable performance evaluations, higher pay and more support from their supervisors and coworkers.

After becoming aware of the power of our thoughts and emotions, it is easy to worry when experiencing negative ones. It is important to accept that negative emotions are part of being human, and at times they are appropriate and necessary. To stay empowered, your goal is not to completely avoid negative thoughts and emotions, but rather to minimize them and strike the right balance.

In fact, research by Fredrickson and Losada (2005) confirms that individuals who flourish in life have a ratio of 3 positive emotions to each negative emotion. In any given day you may not meet this ratio, but over the course of a week or month it is best to strive to do so. In addition, Losada (1999) evaluated the performance of business teams using profitability, customer satisfaction and evaluations by supervisors, peers, and subordinates. Low performing teams' ratios were well below 1 positive to 1 negative and those with good-performance were around 3 to 1. The highest performing teams had high positivity ratios at about 6 to 1. The investigators found that the lowest performing teams were often inflexible and self absorbed. Whereas, high performing teams, raised questions, advocated for each other and were open to new ideas. This culture enabled them to be resilient in the face of adversity and strongly contributed to their success.

> *Within business teams, higher levels of expressed positivity among members have been linked to greater behavioral variability within moment to moment interactions as well as to long range indicators of business success.*
>
> **Marcial Losada and Emily Heaphy, 2004**

At this point you may be wondering if people are just born either positive or negative. Science has determined that our mindset is within our control and that we have opportunities to increase our levels of happiness by how we *think* and what we *do* on a daily basis (Lyubomirsky, 2007). It turns out that empowered successful people have routine ways of thinking and feeling. The good news is that these habits can be learned and cultivated by taking action. *mPWR*[10] is a practical and powerful way to embed the six proven habits into your subconscious mind so that you maintain an empowered mindset, perform consistently at your best and produce the results you want in your life.

SIX *mPWR*[10] HABITS

mPWR
IO®

SIX *mPWR¹⁰* HABITS

mPWR¹⁰ Habits Proven Essential for Success

ere's how you can take the action required to create these habits. By completing the *mPWR¹⁰* tool each day, you will be applying proven, practical techniques that enable you to create new neural pathways in your brain and embed the habits into your subconscious mind. In the back of this book, you will find 30 days of the tool. This small investment of time – just 10 minutes of reflection time each day will allow you to stay 'in control' amidst change and uncertainty; focus on important priorities; generate more creative solutions and reach goals more easily despite challenges. Quickly, the *mPWR¹⁰* habits will become routine and you will be using them automatically throughout your day. As these habits become your habits, you will be shifting your mindset and transforming your results in all areas of your life.

> *We are what we repeatedly do. Excellence, then, is not an act, but a habit.*
> **Aristotle**

The scientifically-proven *mPWR¹⁰* habits

1. Create Goal Momentum
2. Focus on What's Good
3. Pre-Play Events
4. Shift to Positive Interpretations
5. Give and Serve
6. Have FUN!

Create Goal Momentum

From the time we are born, we are goal-driven. Babies learn how to talk and how to walk. When they fall down, they don't think 'Gosh, what if I never walk?' They get right back up and keep going. We start out with big dreams, but somewhere along the way we forget the importance of staying focused on our goals. Life can get so busy and we have so many things going on that we forget our most important priorities.

This habit 'Create Goal Momentum' helps us break through all the clutter in our minds, so that we're in touch with and achieve what we most want – both personally and professionally. This first habit is designed to help you accelerate the pace at which you reach your most meaningful goals.

Written goals are a key driver of personal and professional success. With this focused yet simple process, you will be able to reach your goals like never before and get in the habit of setting and achieving goals more routinely. For creating goal momentum, we encourage you to think of goals that are important to you and with daily energy and focus could be achieved in the next 30 days. If you have a longer-term goal, consider setting a shorter-term milestone.

Here are a few examples of goals that *mPWR*[10] users have created. There are frequently tangible goals such as the sales representative who wanted to be the year-end award winner and chose the short-term monthly goal "I have two new lucrative accounts" to help her get there. A marketing leader chose the goal "I have created and gained strong endorsement of my strategic plan." Often goals can be focused on enhancing a trait or attribute. For example, one sales manager chose an *mPWR*[10] goal "I am a patient father, husband and leader" and another "I am calm and confident in the face of uncertainty and challenge." They both felt that emulating these qualities would enhance their overall leadership strength and ability to achieve sales objectives, as well as significantly benefit those around them. Other *mPWR*[10] users have commonly selected a physical or health-related goal such as "I worked out four times per week this month" or "I have completed a half marathon." Remember, it's most important to select a goal that is motivating and exciting to you that you can get behind and stay on track to achieve.

> *Unless you have definite, precise, clearly set goals, you are not going to realize the maximum potential that lies within you.*
>
> **Zig Ziglar**

To learn the process, you can begin with one or two goals. Most people can name them quickly off the top of their head. Perhaps it is a career or financial goal, a personal health goal, or a relationship goal. Choose two foundation goals that are most important to you right now and will positively impact many other aspects of your life when you achieve them. It is possible to have goals but decide that now is not the ideal time to focus on them. It is important to select goals to which you are absolutely ready to give attention, invest energy and take action.

Once you have selected a goal, write it down as a goal statement and express it as if it has already happened. For example, instead of "I *want* to improve my work-life balance," this goal would be stated as "I *have* great work-life balance and engagement with my family." When we write our goals this way, we begin telling our subconscious minds that we have achieved it and importantly, we begin to *'act as if'* by changing our actions to be consistent with the goal. Also consider and list as many reasons and benefits for achieving the goal. Listing all the benefits of achieving the goal is an ideal way to give you motivation and sustain momentum along the way.

What I most want to achieve in my life right now	Benefits Of Achieving It, Including How It Will Feel To Have It List as many as possible.

Here's the science that supports the three-step goal momentum habit. A total of 267 participants from a variety of industries and backgrounds were recruited for a four-week study (Matthews, 2007). They were randomized to one of five groups. Group one was asked to think about the goals they would like to accomplish over the next four weeks. Group two was asked to write their goals. In addition to writing their goals, group three was also asked to formulate action commitments. Group four was also asked to send their goals and action commitments to a friend. Finally, group five was also asked to weekly provide their progress to a friend. At the end of four weeks, participants rated their success in achieving their goals. Group one members who simply thought about their goals achieved 43% of them. Those in the other groups that were asked to write their goals achieved 64% of them. Group five members who wrote their goals, had actions, celebrated progress and shared with a friend, created the highest level of success achieving 76% of their stated goals.

Clearly the data supports the benefits of writing goals and tracking actions and progress to enhance success. The create goal momentum habit will enable you to easily do this to accelerate achieving what you want.

During your *mPWR[10]* time each day repeat and write your committed goal on your *mPWR[10]* tool. You should continue to write the same goal each day until you achieve it. Repeating your goal daily is a powerful way to tap into your subconscious mind, increase confidence and remove doubt.

With strong emotional involvement in your goal, you don't need to know exactly how it will unfold. Just take a step forward and you will quickly find that amazingly the right events, people and circumstances continue to come into your life inspiring you to take additional steps.

Be assured that having doubt is a very natural part of the process – don't let that deter you! Here are several ways to reduce limiting thoughts and doubts and enhance confidence.

First keep in mind the story of Roger Bannister. Back in the 1950s, most leading scientists strongly believed that it was not and never would be humanly possible to run a mile in under four minutes. At the time, Bannister was certainly a fast miler at approximately 4:11 but even so, he was not ranked among the world's top ten. However Bannister believed that if he continued to focus and train, he would eventually break the four-minute milestone. He improved and then plateaued at 4:05, reinforcing the idea that four minutes could not be broken. Determined, Bannister kept working on his goal and he finally ran the mile in 3:59. What's even more remarkable is that breaking the 4:00 record led to new possibilities for all other runners. Just six weeks later, a man ran the mile in 3:58, and within 18 months an additional 150 runners broke four minutes. When you face obstacles en route to your goal, use this story as motivation to keep going.

Joseph Dowling, the specialist in Peak Performance Psychology, provides another effective technique for enhancing confidence. He recommends utilizing doubt and limiting beliefs to generate solutions. For example, 'What if I fail?' triggers us to ask 'What will it be like when I achieve my goal?' The 'Why is this happening to me?' reminds us to think 'What can I do differently to change my patterns?' The self-critical voice is transformed into a self-supporting inner monologue. Ask yourself how you would talk to a loved one, like a child or valued friend, who wanted to achieve a particular goal…enjoy treating yourself the same way (Dowling, 2009).

It is also important to recognize and accept that challenges and obstacles are part of the process in achieving any meaningful goal. Thomas Edison tried over 3000 experiments before inventing the long-lasting electric light bulb. Fortunately, he confidently persisted and learned from the early failures. Decide from the onset that you will enjoy the journey by turning setbacks into stepping stones and getting back up when you fall down. When facing difficulties, ask yourself what you are learning from the experience and then celebrate that knowledge because it is moving you toward your goal.

After you write your goal on the *mPWR[10]* tool, step two is to record any progress – including small steps you made – to reinforce your momentum and create more of it. Celebrate positive action steps as well as your ability to effectively handle and learn from problems. Both move you closer to your goals! Take note of progress. Depending on your goal, your progress may come in many forms, for example, a salary raise, a great work accomplishment, a wonderful time with your partner or children, a great tennis match or golf outing. Documenting progress increases your confidence that you are moving in the right direction and accelerates the achievement of your goals.

Success is the sum of small efforts, repeated day in and day out.

Robert Collier

The final step in the create goal momentum habit is to take a moment and consider the best next action step to take to keep you moving toward your goal. How do you know if an action is the right one? You will know for sure which actions to take by paying careful attention to how you feel. You will feel inspired or motivated, rather than forced or challenged. You will feel like you are going with the flow rather than fighting the current. Reflection can be incredibly beneficial because it allows us to listen to the wisdom inside of ourselves. We all seek input from those we trust, but it is important to remember to take advice from yourself too, since only you know what is best for you. During *mPWR¹⁰* time, sit quietly and think about the next best step to take toward your goal. Wait patiently and write down what comes to mind. Over time this will empower you to tap into and trust your intuition with greater certainty. Listen to what you wrote down. Consider your guidance and let it inspire your next steps.

Use the space below to practice now.

Create Goal Momentum:

Goal (as if achieved): _______________________

____

Note progress: ___________________________

Next steps: ______________________________

____

____

When we take time to reflect, we often know what we need to do. The answers are within us. The discipline to listen is critical.

John Izzo,
The Five Secrets You Must Discover Before You Die

Experiences of mPWR[10] Users

"Writing my goals keeps me confident and focused on exactly what I need to do that day. By using it, I achieved my goal and became a Major League baseball player." **– Mike C.**

"During a challenging time of transformation in my professional world, I was able to focus my energy on my goals and daily activity rather than the negative energy that was on everyone's mind. One of my goals was to be in the top 5% for my lead product; I reached my goal and am ranked 2nd position in the nation. Overall, mPWR[10] helped me take better control of my day by planning things that were going to take me closer to my goal and pre-playing events prior to going to my appointments." **– Karen R.**

"If not for this terrific program finishing my college degree in Legal Studies would not have happened. This program was also instrumental in helping me cope with the effects of PTSD that I faced as a US Marine." **– Larry S.**

"With mPWR[10] I learned how to approach my goals in bite-size steps, which made them feel more manageable. As a result, I was able to achieve both of the short-term goals I set. Giving my goals attention, energy and focus each day allowed me to prioritize the most important tasks and ask for only what was needed from people. Distractions became less and I made daily progress and felt more confident with each day." **– Marci H.**

*"Since beginning mPWR[10], our company has experienced phenomenal growth. We went from doing about $1M in revenue and we're now at $10M annually. Here's how: mPWR[10] helped me crystallize my goal, where I was going and reasons for not going in other directions. It helped me filter out and gave me permission without guilt to say no to all the activities that I had been doing that weren't going to lead me to my goals and focus each day on the key activities that will take me there." – **George G.***

*"I injured myself playing basketball, which I enjoy doing four to five times per week. Using goal momentum, I'm pushing my rehabilitation to get me back sooner. I've celebrated being on the elliptical without a brace and based on the progress I've made in the past two weeks, I should be able to run next week." – **Tyler N.***

*"I incorporated the mPWR[10] program into my daily life, in literally 10 minutes per day, and it enables me to keep my mind and life moving in the right direction. I have lost 40 pounds and am back in shape. I am now so grateful for the person I am today, and I fully appreciate the special people and experiences I have in my life. The rewards you receive from this small investment of time are incredible!" – **Robert S.***

Now you've listed a meaningful goal, let's turn now to the next five proven habits of success that will support your ability to stay on track, and handle the inevitable obstacles along the way with ease so that you can reach your goal quickly.

Focus on What's Good

hen we are grateful, we train our minds to focus on what is good. It is nearly impossible to find successful people who do not have an extraordinary amount of gratitude. Gratitude always precedes success!

In a study conducted by Emmons and McCullough (2003, 2009), 197 people were randomly assigned to one of three groups. Members of group one were asked to record what they were grateful for, the second group listed hassles of daily life and the third group wrote about random life events. The results were dramatic. Over two months, those that kept gratitude journals exercised 33% more often, reported fewer physical symptoms, felt better about their lives, and were more optimistic about the upcoming week. They were also more likely to have made progress toward important personal goals. Now there's real incentive for actively becoming more grateful.

When we accept things in our lives and are grateful, we let go of resistance and tension. You may not be happy with everything about your current circumstances.

> *When we accept ourselves exactly as we are and where we are, we have more energy to give to life. As soon as we have learned to live most brightly in our present conditions, new and better ones will arrive immediately.*
>
> **Marianne Williamson,**
> *The Gift of Change: Spiritual Guidance for Living your Best Life*

However, by accepting and focusing on what is working well in your life, you are empowered to move forward with solutions. For example, you may want a new job, but it is important to start by remembering what is positive about your current one. Or you may want to achieve better health, but remember all the positive things your body does for you now. When taking on a personal or business challenge, begin by evaluating what is working well and take accountability for moving forward and generating creative solutions for enhancing the business. Think of focusing on what's good as making deposits into your emotional bank account so that when facing inevitable challenges and obstacles, you are able to remain empowered, resilient, in control and stay on track.

Perhaps you are already optimistic and wondering how focusing on what's good will really enhance your results. Think about the news headlines you read or heard today on the internet, newspaper or radio. Consider the obstacles you face daily at work or in your personal life. Each day we are hit with negative influences that challenge our positivity, resilience, and our ability to handle adversity and stay on track to our goals. By building the habit of focusing on what's good, you are creating a built-in shield or buffer to the negative influences that inevitably arise in all our lives.

> *Help people reach their full potential. Catch them doing something right.*
>
> **Kenneth Blanchard and Spencer Johnson,** *The One Minute Manager*

Throughout the day we are faced with many situations that can either be energy drains or energy gains. The choice is ours at every moment. Therefore, when faced with a difficult situation, turn it around by identifying what is working to increase positive emotions and energy to create solutions.

In order to cultivate the habit of focusing on what is good each day, list on the *mPWR¹⁰* tool five things that are going well in your life right now or that happened recently that you are grateful for. Many times these are simple blessings often overlooked in life, or they could be your talents and strengths. For example, the list could include a fun time with family and friends, a great sales call with an important customer, a conversation with a helpful colleague, or even just waking up in the morning and seeing the sunshine. You will soon realize that it is the little things in everyday life, not the big events, that make you happy. Being aware of the things that bring you joy allows you to remember to experience them more often.

As you reflect on gratitude and focus on the good in your life you will feel empowered. Your mind will consistently be open to the many possibilities and solutions and more things to be grateful for will amazingly show up in your life. You will be living in the moment. You can also share with a friend one thing each day for which you are grateful which will create a ripple effect of positive feelings.

Use the space below to practice now.

Focus on What's Good: Things I am grateful for and/or are going well. Consider and include small specific things as well as strengths used.

1 ____

2 ____

3 ____

4 ____

5 ____

Experiences of mPWR[10] Users

"The Focus on What's Good habit has allowed me to have a more positive take on things. The idea that I can have balance in my life is much better. In fact, I feel more productive." **– Kathy F.**

"As a college baseball player, I created a two-minute video clip of my best hitting performances and I replay it to magnify what's good. Watching it immediately lifts me up and keeps me focused." **– Jim C.**

"When I'm facing a challenge, I start by considering what's working well in the situation rather than completely dwelling on the obstacles. I find that this energizes and motivates me and so often I quickly generate creative solutions." **– Brian M.**

"My company recently changed sales quotas without advance warning. I focused on what's good rather than the negative and spiraling down. I stayed positive and thus productive. Now I believe that despite the changes, I will continue to be very successful." **– Carli F.**

"Over the past year, using the Focus on What's Good habit has helped me keep business meetings on track. When I realize we are getting stuck on one agenda item or perhaps ruminating too much on the negative, I pause and ask a simple question such as, 'what's working well in this situation?' I'm amazed at how quickly following this simple technique, we're focusing on actions steps to move us forward." **– Erin B.**

*"I believe wholeheartedly in mPWR[10]! In the past nine months I have had a lot of changes and transitions which would cause many knees to buckle ... instead I have felt completely blessed and more resilient than ever. I was diagnosed with stage 3 melanoma, got married, moved and changed jobs within the company in a span of two months. Due to lots of prayer and utilizing the simple tool of mPWR[10] regularly, my life is more fulfilling and gratifying than ever." – **Michele S.***

Another valuable exercise to use when you are feeling tension in a personal or professional relationship is to take a few minutes to write down everything you appreciate about the other person. You may be amazed at how much good there is. Since what you focus on expands, even if you begin with only one thing, you will likely find more to appreciate about that person.

Pre-Play Events

Remember that you get what you think about and expect. Some individuals have obsessive thoughts of worry or fear prior to an important event and unintentionally cause results that match those thoughts. Fortunately, you can learn to deliberately create what you want by pre-playing events in advance. Doing so empowers you to take actions consistent with creating the actual experience. This works with everyday activities in which you want to be successful as well as with long-term goals you desire to achieve.

Pre-play (also known as visualization, mental preparation or imagery) has long been an effective technique used by elite athletes to enhance their performance. Famous professional athletes Michael Jordan, Jack Nicklaus, Aaron Rodgers, and many others have been known to go through in their minds in great detail the plays in the game or the shots on the course. Their visions are so vivid that occasionally they can feel the twinge in their muscles. They go on to effectively and confidently create the same experience in the actual competition.

Research has demonstrated this correlation of pre-playing with improved athletic performance. In a study conducted with golfers, imagining positively influenced putting skill (Woolfolk, Parrish, & Murphy,

1985.) Also, combined results from a number of sports studies shows that mental practice produces superior learning compared with no practice, and the combination of mental and physical practice appears to be maximally effective for honing skills and making progress (Feltz & Landers, 1983.) Pre-playing events is also known to increase motivation needed to achieve the goal. For example, a study completed by Martin and Hall (1995) concluded that golfers who used visualization set higher goals, spent more time practicing and adhered to their training programs better than those who did not visualize.

Fortunately, the benefits of pre-playing extend beyond sports. In a study conducted by Taylor, Pham, Rivkin & Armor (1998), seventy-seven students were randomized to one of three groups. For a few minutes during each of the five days preceding an exam, the first group was asked to visualize themselves studying in a way that would lead to receiving an A and successfully achieving the A (Process group). This group was instructed to imagine all the details of their studying such as what information they would be reviewing, when, where and with whom they would study, and what potential obstacles would get in the way of fitting in study time, etc. The process group was also asked to imagine and feel the positive emotions of achieving the A. The second group was asked to imagine themselves having gotten an A and feeling proud and confident upon receiving the news (Outcome group). There was also a control group that was given no

> *Most successful people have developed this ability, through practice, to create clear, vivid mental pictures of themselves being the persons and doing the things they really want.*
>
> Brian Tracy, *Maximum Achievement: Strategies and Skills That Will Unlock Your Hidden Powers to Succeed.*

instruction and they simply monitored their studying over the same period prior to the exam. Those in the Process group studied more and added 8 points to their score relative to the control group. The Outcome group members who just visualized the outcome of receiving an A actually studied fewer days and hours which contributed to their lower score. Pre-playing gave the Process group advantages for three primary reasons. First, pre-playing enabled them to anticipate challenges and allowed their subconscious mind to provide solutions for handling these obstacles, such as finding times and places to study. Second, pre-playing gave them the motivation to study and take the necessary actions to achieve the end result. Finally, they were more prepared and their confidence was enhanced, making them feel relaxed and poised going into the exam. Thus the key is to imagine and feel the details of the event unfolding, as well as the outcome that you are trying to achieve.

If you want to make healthier choices, here's another study demonstrating how pre-playing can dramatically improve your likelihood of success. Knäuper et al (2011) asked 177 participants to set themselves the goal of consuming more fruit for a period of seven days. One of the groups in the study was instructed to do two additional things: write an action plan of how, when and where they'd buy and eat more fruit and visualize themselves carrying out their plan. This group imagined not only eating more fruit, but how it would smell, feel, look and taste. At the end of seven days, all participants had consumed more fruit than they had beforehand. However, the group that made a concrete plan and visualized carrying it out increased their fruit consumption twice as much as those who simply set out to eat more fruit.

You can pre-play to enhance any aspect of your life, from customer interactions to vacations to tennis serves or conversations with your child, spouse or coworker. For example, if you have an upcoming customer meeting imagine yourself confidently presenting. Think through the challenging questions and objections that you may be asked and feel yourself responding effectively. Feel the supportive and receptive tone of your audience. By preparing in this manner you will be using your subconscious mind to help you anticipate and prepare to effectively cope with challenges. And when things get thrown your way that you did not pre-play, you will be able to effectively handle them because your mind is open and can easily access the best answers and solutions.

To get in the habit of pre-playing events, each day choose something for which you desire a successful outcome. This may be a step related to your goal but doesn't have to be. First, list the details of the event on your *mPWR*[10] tool. Then, take a few deep breaths and visualize, imagine and feel the specifics unfolding and leading to positive outcomes. You want your mental pictures to approximate the actual experience as closely as possible, so see yourself speaking, feeling and acting exactly as you want to be. As you imagine the details, you will be tapping into your subconscious mind and generating ways to handle challenges and productive actions you can take to reach your desired outcome.

Use the space below to practice now.

Pre-play events: List below the details, including effectively handling potential obstacles and a positive outcome. Then, visualize the event.

____

____

____

Experiences of mPWR[10] Users

"I had to give a presentation and learned that senior management was going to attend. I used the pre-play habit to visualize the details – when to gain feedback, how to engage the audience and interject questions, etc. I thought I would be nervous, but I felt extremely prepared and confident as if it were the second time I was delivering the presentation and the presentation went just as I envisioned!" **– Joanne D.**

"As a minor league baseball player, pre-playing helps me concentrate on being positive and trusting myself to succeed, rather than being over-analytical." **– Peter H.**

"I pre-played prior to a meeting with my team to communicate a company reorganization. I wanted to ensure they felt heard and knew that I have their best interest in mind. I anticipated many of their concerns and questions. I felt well prepared and the meeting could not have gone better." **– Laura R.**

"I now routinely use the pre-play habit. I had an important call with a group of cardiologists that I was conducting with a teammate. While pre-playing, I got an idea for a compelling opening using a video animation and thought through how to coordinate the call between my teammate and I to ensure a successful outcome. As a result, I felt confident and relaxed and the call went great. My teammate even sent a text to my manager commenting on how prepared I was." **– Maurice D.**

"I had an interview for a new position that would enable me to continue to grow within the company. I was feeling at a disadvantage because I was to interview by phone while the other candidates interviewed in person. I decided to take the time to write out the details and visualize the best possible impression I could make and how to convey it in a compelling way by phone. It was a great interview and I'm happy to say I got the job." **– Tom R.**

"Before every At-Bat, I close my eyes and imagine myself hitting the ball and being successful. This relaxes me and enhances my confidence." **– A.J.M.**

Shift to Positive Interpretations

nother important way to be more empowered and productive is to make it a habit to assume positive intent and interpret situations more positively. Each day we are faced with big and small challenging or awkward situations. Often these create automatic assumptions that are negative triggering strong emotions which can result in feeling discouraged or defeated. These emotions can lead to unproductive acts or even no action at all. Often, we get distracted and waste valuable time and energy that could be used in more productive ways. Think about how often we quickly jump to negative conclusions based on the statement or action of a stranger, coworker, friend, or spouse before even fully understanding the situation.

For all we know, he or she may be dealing with a personal challenge that has nothing to do with us. How often are we frustrated because we want or expect a person, situation or circumstance to change when it is up to us to change how we respond?

Once you get into the habit of disputing negative beliefs, your daily life will run much better, and you will feel much happier.

Martin Seligman,
Learned Optimism

Highly effective people interpret and respond to adversity with a positive perspective on a routine basis. Research completed by Seligman and Shulman (1986) supports the conclusion that positive interpretations and responses drive success in sales. In their study of Metropolitan Life

Insurance salespeople, agents scoring in the top 50% for optimism sold 37% more than the less optimistic agents in the bottom half of optimism scale. Moreover, those scoring in the top ten percent for optimism sold 88% more than the agents in the bottom ten percent for optimism. In the face of rejection, when some agents felt like giving up, more optimistic agents believed that upcoming calls were likely to be productive and were motivated to continue. When reflecting on an inevitable setback, successful salespeople routinely evaluate what went well, what they learned and productive actions they can use when approaching future meetings.

Shifting to positive interpretations alters your emotions, leading to more rational decision-making and outcomes that are likely to be productive. So this habit can be described as hitting the PAUSE BUTTON. Stop in the moment when you feel negative emotions and identify an alternative interpretation. Ask yourself why else might this person be behaving the way they are or why else might this situation be as it is. For example, perhaps your manager calls you in for an impromptu meeting. Rather than worrying that you have done something wrong or that there is a problem, anticipate a positive collaborative meeting. If you receive an email from the assistant of an important customer canceling an appointment to meet with you, rather than assuming the customer is uninterested in your product or service, pause and ask yourself what else could have caused the cancellation. Through that simple question you will generate multiple possibilities and feel empowered to move forward in productive ways. To create the results they want, successful people

> *Life is 10% what happens to you and 90% how you react to it.*
>
> **Charles R. Swindoll**

habitually look for constructive information to identify alternative possibilities to shift their thinking when challenges arise in their lives.

After shifting to more empowered emotions, ask yourself, "what productive actions can I take to achieve the results I want?" This will allow you to generate creative solutions to move forward. For example, when your boss gives you feedback on a business presentation or report, instead of thinking that you are not very talented and will not get promoted, remind yourself of your history of success and the praise your boss typically gives your work. Then work diligently to incorporate the comments and get the document back to her quickly. Imagine her commending the final result. When you have missed your workout routine for three days and feel incredibly guilty, how can you shift to a more positive interpretation? Remind yourself that you are still healthy and just need to get back on track by taking a few challenging classes at the gym this week, or by eating healthy and cutting back calories for the next week, or by taking a walk after work.

Accept the fact that you cannot change what has already happened. Nor can you change someone else. You can only change yourself and how you respond. So get in the habit of challenging these automatic negative thoughts and instead shift to positive interpretations about yourself and others. This will minimize distractions and maximize your ability to stay focused on what you want.

To cultivate the habit of shifting to positive interpretations, begin to challenge negative conclusions or thoughts you have about a situation, yourself or another person. On your *mPWR*[10] tool list alternative possibilities and then productive actions you can take to move forward and stay productive. By completing the tool, you will be tapping into your subconscious mind and generating new ideas and possibilities for how to overcome the challenge. As you practice and build this habit, you will find yourself shifting automatically and consistently staying empowered and on track.

Use the space below to practice now.

Shift to Positive Interpretations: Pause and challenge negative interpretations about yourself, situations and others.

Alternative Possibilities: _______________________________

____

____

Productive Actions: _________________________________

____

____

Experiences of mPWR[10] Users

*"mPWR[10] is a great framework that makes me think a bit differently. The habit of shift to positive interpretations has had the most profound impact. I find that I am more generous to peoples' intent by stepping back and really putting myself in their position, which has meant better outcomes for both parties." – **Lee E.***

*"This habit helped me shift from beating myself up to being self-supportive. My mantra after a mistake on the court is, "The next play is the first play." Using this technique in college helped me reach my full potential and excel on the basketball court." – **Jon J.***

"I planned a meeting with 300 key customers to be trained to speak on the company's behalf. As you can imagine, an extraordinary amount of work went into planning the event. Just ten days before the program, after all the travel, logistics and content were complete, senior management stated that we had to cut the number of attendees to 150. I knew this habit was working when my colleagues noticed that I remained calm, didn't complain about the decision, instead shifted my energy to brainstorming on how to make the most out of this situation and create a positive solution."
– Patrick D.

"I had a client that was short with me and I was worried that he was pulling his business. I used the shift habit to consider other reasons for the customer's behavior. For example, perhaps he was having a bad day and it had nothing to do with me. Then, my productive action was to focus on the client's needs and do the best I could to continue to bring high-quality service. My subsequent interactions were much more positive and in fact, our business with this client is thriving." *– Joe S.*

"We've reorganized and I'm working with a new unfamiliar boss and colleagues. Regularly shifting to positive interpretations has helped me keep a good perspective when feeling uncertain about some of the things they say and do. As a result, I'm able to stay focused, collaborative and productive." *– Laura R.*

"This habit has helped me tremendously. I was given very short notice for a business trip that meant considerable air travel and conflicted with a weekend trip away. I used the shift to positive interpretations habit and reframed the situation by choosing to see it as an opportunity. I used it as an opportunity to network and make a positive impact on the project. As a result, I was in a good frame of mind and well prepared!" *– Susan T.*

"I began using the mPWR^{10} program to enhance my family relationships. I have a couple of difficult siblings that I love dearly, but I realized that for a long time I had too many expectations of them. The shift to positive interpretations habit has really made a difference and leads me to challenge negative interpretations I make about myself and others. It has really helped me see the good in my siblings and celebrate them. I found that when I did that my relationships got easier, more loving, and our time together as a family is now fantastic."
– Dave R.

"It makes so much sense to talk to myself the same way I talk to my football teammates – positive and reassuring without acknowledging any doubt." **– Ryan K.**

Give and Serve

 e also refer to this habit as other-mindedness, putting others first or paying it forward. Jim Collins and his colleagues spent more than ten years studying and analyzing how great companies achieve superior performance, grow and then perform consistently well over time. In the best-selling book, *Good To Great*, Jim Collins identified humility as the hallmark attribute of truly great leaders. For these leaders, it was never about them, nor were they driven by their own ego. Rather they consistently thought about and acted in ways that supported others and put them first. As a result, they inspired, motivated and enhanced others' performance and growth. To be a great role model and/or leader in your personal and professional life, create the habit of giving and serving others daily.

> Leadership is helping others get what they want.
>
> **Harvey Jackson**

The correlation between recording acts of kindness and increasing positive emotions was demonstrated by Otake et al (2006). In this study participants were asked to track acts of kindness they performed during one week. There was also a comparison group that did not track acts of kindness. Subjective happiness was measured one month prior to the start of the study and one month after the end. Those that recorded acts of kindness experienced a significant increase in happiness scores, but the comparison group did not. In addition, a subgroup with the biggest increase in happiness reported performing more kind behaviors, and in the process also became more grateful. Keep in mind these benefits were demonstrated after *just one week*. Imagine how making giving and serving a routine habit can benefit your life!

When you give back or serve others you automatically help yourself because it feels good to help others. When you give to others, you immediately take your focus off of your problems or worries. By doing so you will find that your connections with them grow stronger. Also, helping others highlights your abilities and values, which is a wonderful way to enhance your self-confidence and reduce your stress.

A mentality of scarcity causes us to hold tightly to things. However, a mentality of abundance and the act of service creates space for more good to come into your world. People often say, "I am too busy, I don't have time." Focusing on what you *can* do will position you for success and generate a mindset of abundance. In essence, when you believe you have enough time to do what you need to and time to spend with those you care for, you create a space for it. You are empowered. How you spend your time is your choice.

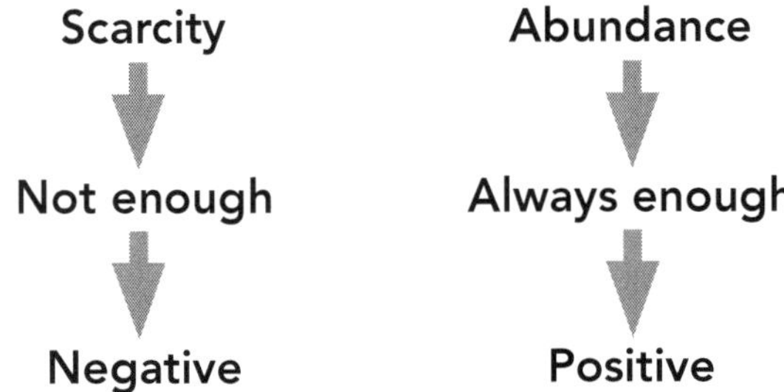

If you want to instantly lift your spirits and raise your self-esteem, find a way to help another person. Each day ask yourself how you can provide service to others. It can be simple, perhaps even unnoticed. The intent should be to do something positive or helpful for someone else without expecting that you will receive anything in return. Even the smallest gesture can mean so much to someone, and you will find you gain much more than you give. Here are some examples of how you can start giving and serving right now.

> It's amazing how much can be accomplished if no one cares who gets the credit.
>
> **John Wooden, *Legendary Coach of UCLA Men's Basketball***

Give your colleague a heart-felt compliment.

Support a person who is experiencing a tough life challenge.

Give a chance to people who are sincere.

Send a positive message to a friend in need.

Volunteer in your community.

Listen to and support a teammate.

Say hello and offer a smile to the receptionist.

Let a stranger go ahead of you in line at the grocery store.

Offer to mentor someone.

Pitch in to help a colleague with a work project.

Bring dinner to a family in need.

Take a colleague to lunch.

Recognize colleagues/staff for their work.

Make time for a colleague who asks you to review something.

Some people feel an obligation or duty to serve and do so with negative emotion because they really

> *It is one of the most beautiful compensations of this life that no man can sincerely try to help another without helping himself.*
>
> **Ralph Waldo Emerson**

don't feel like doing it. Instead, if we reframe the simple everyday tasks we do for others and perform them with more sincerity, we emit positive emotions which allow us to create more of what we want in our lives, while at the same time have a ripple effect on others.

Use the space below to practice now.

Give and Serve: Ways I can add value and focus on others.

____

____

____

____

Experiences of mPWR[10] Users

*"Using mPWR[10] over the last few months is an outstanding way to support the high-performing behaviors and focus on personal development that we want to embed in our business unit. By starting my day with the program, my key priorities stay top of mind. I've enjoyed using the give and serve habit to remind me to highlight and celebrate wins of individuals on my team." – **Matt B.***

*"I found that by shifting focus on the customer rather than my sales objectives, and considering what the customer wants, enabled our interactions to be much more engaging and enjoyable. As a result, I'm helping the customer and in the end this has led to quicker and increased sales." – **Chad D.***

"I'm applying give/serve to be more authentically focused on my customers' goals and needs. I'm finding that the energy with customers is even more positive." **– Eric K.**

"When I focus on my college basketball teammates and build them up, I feel better as a person and we all play better." **– Mark G.**

"The habit Give and Serve has made a big impact on how I lead. Every Friday I have 30 minutes scheduled as dedicated time to appreciate my team by writing thank you notes or emails and this had had a very positive impact on their motivation and outlook." **– Kerry M.**

Have FUN!

reate the habit of doing at least one thing just for you each day that evokes positive emotions. We live in a very busy world with jam-packed days. It seems as if we are running 24/7. Do you routinely do things just for yourself that allow you to briefly escape and focus on you and your needs? It is common for busy people to make the mistake of not scheduling breaks in their day because of the perspective that their other responsibilities don't leave time for it. However, when we neglect ourselves we may feel depleted and stressed. Building relaxation and having fun helps us recharge and actually makes us more productive. So carve out time for one thing each day that means "fun" to you, that is not an obligation or duty.

A study by Diener, Nickerson, Lucas, and Sandvik (2000) showed that positive emotions contribute to higher incomes. In addition, combined results from nearly 300 studies concluded that positive emotions enhance both success and health (Lyubomirsky, King, & Diener, 2005).

According to Joseph Dowling, specialist in Peak Performance Psychology, the definition of fun is a brief opportunity to become completely absorbed; a timeless place when you forget the to-do list and any concerns or worry. It may be the runners' high of aerobic exercise or mindfulness of yoga, or maybe it is becoming engrossed in a great novel or movie. Perhaps you get lost while painting or taking a dance class. Other great outlets are sports that require concentration such as golf, tennis, or basketball. Your fun may be taking a walk in nature or spending time with your partner or friends. Whatever it is, experience some form of it each day and you will boost your resilience.

Another way to maximize the value of your fun time is to 'plant seeds.' The next time you're struggling with a challenge, calmly ask for the answer in the form of a question and then forget about the problem and go do something fun. Then while you are absorbed in the activity, you are creating positive emotions and your subconscious mind is able to work on the question. So many people are amazed at the inspired ideas that come to them from seemingly 'out of the blue.' By routinely building this $mPWR^{10}$ habit, you will have more energy and find yourself more focused and productive.

> *More than any other element, fun is the secret to Virgin's success. This isn't just because fun is well fun. It's because fun also leads to bottom-line results.*
>
> **Richard Branson, *CEO Virgin Group* *as quoted in Delivering Happiness* *by Tony Hsieh***

Use the space below to practice now.

Have FUN!: What can I do just for fun, to recharge.

____

____

Experiences of mPWR[10] Users

"I used to feel guilty about dedicating time to do things for myself because it meant taking time away from my family and other responsibilities. However, committing to what I will do for myself and then actually following through made me realize just how beneficial it is and how much of a difference it makes." – **Maria B.**

"I have always been career-driven and felt a bit guilty and indulgent if I took time away from work responsibilities for myself. I realized that I needed to build in fun with my family. By scheduling in fun, I have found that I enjoy life so much more AND it has actually made me more effective in my job." – **Kim G.**

"Integrating fun into my daily work life was something I did not allow myself to do. I left it for weekends. mPWR[10] has given me the permission to plan my day and reward myself. At a minimum, I build a break into my day and I am amazed at how much more effective I am versus the George I was six months ago. By giving myself permission to have fun, I have truly sharpened my ax and become more focused." – **George G.**

mPWR¹⁰ Reflection Time – 10 Minutes a Day

Now it's time to plan for your success. How you decide to use the *mPWR¹⁰* program is flexible and up to you. Right now you may be motivated to invest 10 minutes a day and apply these habits using the *mPWR¹⁰* tool. If so, you will likely find that these habits will become your habits and you'll be using them automatically throughout your day. The *mPWR¹⁰* tool is so effective because it is a structured framework that enables you to practice all six of these habits in just 10 minutes. Also, writing acts as a filter for the brain and gives importance to what you're actively focusing on and diminishes distractions. Another great way to jumpstart the program is to commit to 10 minutes a day for 10 days to get a sense for the value *mPWR¹⁰* can have for you.

A tip is to identify the same time each day when you will complete your tool, so that it becomes routine. Many do so in the morning, before their day gets busy. This allows them to 'set a positive tone' and stay on track. Find a time that will work for you.

Keep in mind this is not an all or nothing program. As you have seen, all of the habits are proven to drive success so using any of them more routinely can have a profound impact on your life. Perhaps, you identified a habit or two that you believe would enhance your life significantly. If that's the case, go ahead and incorporate those habits more consistently and see the benefits, personally and/or professionally.

Should you find that get off track, it is also very easy to resume using *mPWR¹⁰* to get back on track! We hope that you find like so many others that *mPWR¹⁰* can help you be more consistently at your best and achieve meaningful goals in all areas of your life.

Experiences of mPWR[10] Users:
Dave, Pharmaceutical Sales Manager

The reason I got started with mPWR[10] in the first place was because I have read many books over the years about the power of a positive mindset. So I believed in the concept and this program intrigued me. What kept me going was the simplicity of the program. Instead of continually reading new material, I found something that finally brought it all together for me AND produced results. Today I spend 10 minutes every morning and I'm thrilled with the changes I have experienced both personally and professionally.

What has changed in my life is incredible actually. It began with golf. I'm very passionate about the game and wanted to be great at it. When I started mPWR[10], I was about an 18 handicap, which is average by most standards. I struggled quite a bit on the course. I even walked off in embarrassment and frustration several times. The group that I played with had a lot of fun with me back then, they were very patient.

I created a specific goal of 'I have an eight handicap.' which I wrote each morning. Then I began celebrating progress along the way and determining the specific actions I needed to take to get there. This was always the piece that was missing for me, and it became very clear when I started using the program. Here's what happened. Within 2 months, I had a perfect score of 72 which is the best score I ever shot. After about four months, I got a hole in one, which is extremely cool. In the club house there is a big glass case with trophies behind it. I decided I wanted my name on one of those trophies. During each round, I stayed focused and beat some of the best golfers leading to me becoming the champion of the second biggest tournament at our club. My name is now on one of those trophies. Shortly after, I achieved my goal of an eight handicap. Now I'm down to a six handicap and consistently beat the guys who used to make fun of me.

Once I started seeing incredible results in my golf game, it was a no-brainer to use mPWR[10] in other areas of my life.

Experiences of mPWR[10] Users:
Kathryn, Pharmaceutical Marketing Director

Like so many other people, I have read motivational books and participated in coaching programs in the past, though have never been able to achieve the results I have with mPWR[10]. The program's practical approach allows me to easily integrate it into my busy and crowded life. I start my day with mPWR[10] at home before I leave for work. These few minutes really help me focus and get in the right frame of mind to start my day. I also find it keeps the habits top of mind so that I routinely use them throughout my day.

The habits are easy to follow and within a short period of time I found myself feeling empowered and being more productive professionally and personally. For example, by pausing and shifting to positive interpretations and pre-playing events, I find I am able to bring out the best in most situations. When I encounter a particularly challenging situation or person, I am able to reframe the issue and approach it in more optimistic and productive manner. This has helped me become much more efficient and also has resulted in positive ripple effects for others I work with. I'm now confident that I am equipped to create the outcomes I want in meetings, on work projects and even in my personal relationships.

Since beginning mPWR[10] , I am also much more focused on my overall goals and the steps I need to take on a daily basis to reach them. For example, shortly after beginning the program, I learned that my department was reorganizing and my position was being eliminated. In the past, that would have caused a tremendous fear and anxiety. But I instead focused on what I wanted in a calm assured way. mPWR[10] helped me take the large goal of finding a new desirable job and break it into smaller, manageable components. I had the tools I needed and each day I created momentum and moved closer to it. I am now in a terrific new position. Overall, I'm grateful that I'm able to spread a contagious positive mindset and demeanor now. I've experienced so many positive changes in my life; I'm achieving my goals and enjoying life more than ever.

Experiences of mPWR[10] Users:
Kim, General Manager

I initially became interested in mPWR[10] in hopes that the program could help my business avoid an off year in sales due to the downturn in the economy. mPWR[10] has given me that and so much more. Each morning, before my children awake, I spend time with mPWR[10] while enjoying my coffee to get my day off to a great start! Thinking about and writing down what I'm grateful for, made me FEEL the WOW in my life. I am no longer worried about what I don't have; and I fully appreciate and savor all the good that I do have.

Throughout my days, as challenging situations inevitably arise, I now feel empowered to make changes rather than expecting the situation or others to do so. mPWR[10] works! It's fast! I am amazed at the immediate positive results I've experienced. My confidence has soared which has led me to stretch my comfort zone and try new things on the professional side.

Team members and outside vendors are noticing my optimism, and my positive energy has resulted in a number of new, fruitful business opportunities. mPWR[10] has also had a ripple effect on my team. Also, I have stepped back and encouraged my managers to lead their individual departments, which has empowered them. Despite the difficult retail economy, each of the departments is exceeding their goals.

I don't believe in luck, unless you win the lottery. If you prepare yourself for the next level you will make it happen. I believe that is what mPWR[10] has done for me! As a result, I have taken my personal and professional results to the next level and looking forward to keeping it going!

Experiences of mPWR[10] Users:
Patrick, Marketing Director

I always considered myself a positive and successful person. I often read books on personal growth and leadership, and for many years I have set and achieved personal and professional goals in my life. When asked to use mPWR[10] and provide my insights and feedback, I agreed, not realizing what a dramatic impact it would have in my life!

When I began using the program my company was in the midst of reorganization. I had a lot of anxiety over whether my position was at risk, and I was spending time worrying about what would happen if I lost my job. I quickly realized that thinking about these things that are outside of my control made me considerably less productive. So now, even though down-sizing remains a possibility, I am focused on how I can positively contribute to the organization. As a result I'm much more effective each day.

Since using mPWR[10] for the past year, I've become a much more effective and creative problem solver when facing inevitable work or personal challenges. It has a ripple effect as well. My colleagues have commented that I remain calm and focused and quickly find and drive solutions. Before mPWR[10], negative energy sometimes limited my ability to think through all possible options to solve the problem. My resilience has improved, and I'm confident I will be able to handle with ease whatever situation comes my way.

mPWR[10] definitely has helped create momentum for my goals. I wanted to help redefine the culture within the marketing organization. After just a few months focusing on this goal consistently, I was selected to lead an organization-wide project with a mission to enhance the culture and workforce engagement. Another of my goals was achieving work-life balance, and better engagement with my family. After a few weeks of doing the program, I was leaving the office earlier.

My family has noticed that I am more positive at home, and don't bring the stress of my job responsibilities through the front door. Today my routine includes a few minutes with mPWR[10] as my computer is powering up in the morning. It gives me a chance to focus on all the good there is in my life and what I want to bring about that day. After all the benefits mPWR[10] has brought to my life, I enthusiastically recommend it to others and wouldn't consider not continuing it myself.

m
PWR
IO
mPWR 10 TOOL
mPWR 10 TOOL
mPWR 10 TOOL

m PWR 10

mPWR¹⁰ TOOL

mPWR¹⁰ tool Example   Date _________

Create Goal Momentum:

Goal (as if achieved): _I am healthy, energetic and weigh x pounds_

Note progress: _Made healthy choices for meals yesterday_

____

Next steps: _Arrange to meet a friend to walk at lunch_

Goal: _I am in the top 10% of sales people in my region this month_

Note progress: _Turned a top potential client onto x product today which will boost my sales._

Next steps: _Complete key action steps that came out of yesterday's meeting_

Focus on What's Good: Things for which I am grateful and/or are going well in my life. Consider and include small specific things as well as strengths used.

1 _My family_

2 _Feeling healthy and having good energy when I woke today._

3 _Wonderful telephone conversation catching up with my friend._

4 _Job with benefits_

5 _Amazing weather that allowed me to walk outside at lunch_

Pre-play events: List below the details, including effectively handling potential obstacles and a positive outcome. Then, visualize the event.

Important meeting with a key customer is highly interactive. There is positive energy and good collaborative dialogue throughout. The customer is engaged and expresses high interest. I confidently handle various questions and objections and he is pleased with responses. He is excited to make initial purchase and after trial consider a larger commitment in the future.

Shift to Positive Interpretations: Pause and challenge negative interpretations about yourself, situations and others.

Alternative Possibilities: Perhaps they had something unexpected come up

or aren't feeling well.

Productive Actions: I can use the time to catch up on a few important projects.

I will reschedule the appointment quickly and prepare so that when I have the

appointment it will be great

Give and Serve: Ways I can add value and focus on others.

Read an extra book to my son, help colleague with a work project

Have FUN!: What can I do just for fun, to recharge.

Play tennis, watch my favorite TV show

mPWR¹⁰ tool   Date _______________

Create Goal Momentum:

Goal (as if achieved): _______________________________________

Note progress: _______________________________________

Next steps: _______________________________________

Goal (as if achieved): _______________________________________

Note progress: _______________________________________

Next steps: _______________________________________

Focus on What's Good: Things I am grateful for and/or are going well. Consider and include small specific things as well as strengths used.

1 _______________________________________

2 _______________________________________

3 _______________________________________

4 _______________________________________

5 _______________________________________

Pre-play events: List below the details, including effectively handling potential obstacles and a positive outcome. Then, visualize the event.

____

____

____

Shift to Positive Interpretations: Pause and challenge negative interpretations about yourself, situations and others.

Alternative Possibilities: _______________________________________

____

Productive Actions: _______________________________________

____

Give and Serve: Ways I can add value and focus on others. _______________

____

Have FUN!: What can I do just for fun, to recharge.

____

mPWR¹⁰ tool   Date _________________

Create Goal Momentum:

Goal (as if achieved): ____

Note progress: ____

Next steps: ____

Goal (as if achieved): ____

Note progress: ____

Next steps: ____

Focus on What's Good: Things I am grateful for and/or are going well. Consider and include small specific things as well as strengths used.

1 ____

2 ____

3 ____

4 ____

5 ____

Pre-play events: List below the details, including effectively handling potential obstacles and a positive outcome. Then, visualize the event.

____

____

____

Shift to Positive Interpretations: Pause and challenge negative interpretations about yourself, situations and others.

Alternative Possibilities: ____

____

Productive Actions: ____

____

Give and Serve: Ways I can add value and focus on others. _____________

____

Have FUN!: What can I do just for fun, to recharge.

____

mPWR¹⁰ tool   Date ________________

Create Goal Momentum:

Goal (as if achieved): ____

Note progress: ____

Next steps: ____

Goal (as if achieved): ____

Note progress: ____

Next steps: ____

Focus on What's Good: Things I am grateful for and/or are going well. Consider and include small specific things as well as strengths used.

1 ____

2 ____

3 ____

4 ____

5 ____

Pre-play events: List below the details, including effectively handling potential obstacles and a positive outcome. Then, visualize the event.

____

____

____

Shift to Positive Interpretations: Pause and challenge negative interpretations about yourself, situations and others.

Alternative Possibilities: ____

____

Productive Actions: ____

____

Give and Serve: Ways I can add value and focus on others. _____________

____

Have FUN!: What can I do just for fun, to recharge.

____

mPWR¹⁰ tool　　　　　　　　　Date ________________

Create Goal Momentum:

Goal (as if achieved): ____

Note progress: ____

Next steps: ____

Goal (as if achieved): ____

Note progress: ____

Next steps: ____

Focus on What's Good: Things I am grateful for and/or are going well. Consider and include small specific things as well as strengths used.

1 ____

2 ____

3 ____

4 ____

5 ____

Pre-play events: List below the details, including effectively handling potential obstacles and a positive outcome. Then, visualize the event.

____

____

____

Shift to Positive Interpretations: Pause and challenge negative interpretations about yourself, situations and others.

Alternative Possibilities: _______________________________________

____

Productive Actions: ____

____

Give and Serve: Ways I can add value and focus on others. ______________

____

Have FUN!: What can I do just for fun, to recharge.

____

mPWR[10] tool

Date ___________________

Create Goal Momentum:

Goal (as if achieved): ____

Note progress: ____

Next steps: ____

Goal (as if achieved): ____

Note progress: ____

Next steps: ____

Focus on What's Good: Things I am grateful for and/or are going well. Consider and include small specific things as well as strengths used.

1 ____

2 ____

3 ____

4 ____

5 ____

Pre-play events: List below the details, including effectively handling potential obstacles and a positive outcome. Then, visualize the event.

____

____

____

Shift to Positive Interpretations: Pause and challenge negative interpretations about yourself, situations and others.

Alternative Possibilities: ____

____

Productive Actions: ____

____

Give and Serve: Ways I can add value and focus on others. ________________

____

Have FUN!: What can I do just for fun, to recharge.

____

mPWR¹⁰ tool

Date ___________________

Create Goal Momentum:

Goal (as if achieved): ____

Note progress: ____

Next steps: ____

Goal (as if achieved): ____

Note progress: ____

Next steps: ____

Focus on What's Good: Things I am grateful for and/or are going well. Consider and include small specific things as well as strengths used.

1 ____

2 ____

3 ____

4 ____

5 ____

Pre-play events: List below the details, including effectively handling potential obstacles and a positive outcome. Then, visualize the event.

____

____

____

Shift to Positive Interpretations: Pause and challenge negative interpretations about yourself, situations and others.

Alternative Possibilities: ______________________________________

____

Productive Actions: ____

____

Give and Serve: Ways I can add value and focus on others. _____________

____

Have FUN!: What can I do just for fun, to recharge.

____

mPWR¹⁰ tool Date ___________________

Create Goal Momentum:

Goal (as if achieved): ____

Note progress: ____

Next steps: ____

Goal (as if achieved): ____

Note progress: ____

Next steps: ____

Focus on What's Good: Things I am grateful for and/or are going well. Consider and include small specific things as well as strengths used.

1 ____

2 ____

3 ____

4 ____

5 ____

Pre-play events: List below the details, including effectively handling potential obstacles and a positive outcome. Then, visualize the event.

____

____

____

Shift to Positive Interpretations: Pause and challenge negative interpretations about yourself, situations and others.

Alternative Possibilities: ____

____

Productive Actions: ____

____

Give and Serve: Ways I can add value and focus on others. _______________

____

Have FUN!: What can I do just for fun, to recharge.

____

mPWR¹⁰ tool   Date ________________

Create Goal Momentum:

Goal (as if achieved): ____

Note progress: ____

Next steps: ____

Goal (as if achieved): ____

Note progress: ____

Next steps: ____

Focus on What's Good: Things I am grateful for and/or are going well. Consider and include small specific things as well as strengths used.

1 ____

2 ____

3 ____

4 ____

5 ____

Pre-play events: List below the details, including effectively handling potential obstacles and a positive outcome. Then, visualize the event.

____

____

____

Shift to Positive Interpretations: Pause and challenge negative interpretations about yourself, situations and others.

Alternative Possibilities: ____

____

Productive Actions: ____

____

Give and Serve: Ways I can add value and focus on others. ________________

____

Have FUN!: What can I do just for fun, to recharge.

____

mPWR¹⁰ tool

Date ___________________

Create Goal Momentum:

Goal (as if achieved): ____

Note progress: ____

Next steps: ____

Goal (as if achieved): ____

Note progress: ____

Next steps: ____

Focus on What's Good: Things I am grateful for and/or are going well. Consider and include small specific things as well as strengths used.

1 ____

2 ____

3 ____

4 ____

5 ____

Pre-play events: List below the details, including effectively handling potential obstacles and a positive outcome. Then, visualize the event.

____

____

____

Shift to Positive Interpretations: Pause and challenge negative interpretations about yourself, situations and others.

Alternative Possibilities: ____

____

Productive Actions: ____

____

Give and Serve: Ways I can add value and focus on others. _______________

____

Have FUN!: What can I do just for fun, to recharge.

____

mPWR¹⁰ tool

Date ________________

Create Goal Momentum:

Goal (as if achieved): ______________________________________

Note progress: ____

Next steps: ____

Goal (as if achieved): ______________________________________

Note progress: ____

Next steps: ____

Focus on What's Good: Things I am grateful for and/or are going well. Consider and include small specific things as well as strengths used.

1 ____

2 ____

3 ____

4 ____

5 ____

Pre-play events: List below the details, including effectively handling potential obstacles and a positive outcome. Then, visualize the event.

____

____

____

Shift to Positive Interpretations: Pause and challenge negative interpretations about yourself, situations and others.

Alternative Possibilities: __________________________________

____

Productive Actions: ______________________________________

____

Give and Serve: Ways I can add value and focus on others. _____________

____

Have FUN!: What can I do just for fun, to recharge.

____

mPWR¹⁰ tool

Date _______________

Create Goal Momentum:

Goal (as if achieved): ____

Note progress: ____

Next steps: ____

Goal (as if achieved): ____

Note progress: ____

Next steps: ____

Focus on What's Good: Things I am grateful for and/or are going well. Consider and include small specific things as well as strengths used.

1 ____

2 ____

3 ____

4 ____

5 ____

Pre-play events: List below the details, including effectively handling potential obstacles and a positive outcome. Then, visualize the event.

____

____

____

Shift to Positive Interpretations: Pause and challenge negative interpretations about yourself, situations and others.

Alternative Possibilities: ____

____

Productive Actions: ____

____

Give and Serve: Ways I can add value and focus on others. _______________

____

Have FUN!: What can I do just for fun, to recharge.

____

mPWR¹⁰ tool   Date ________________

Create Goal Momentum:

Goal (as if achieved): ____

Note progress: ____

Next steps: ____

Goal (as if achieved): ____

Note progress: ____

Next steps: ____

Focus on What's Good: Things I am grateful for and/or are going well. Consider and include small specific things as well as strengths used.

1 ____

2 ____

3 ____

4 ____

5 ____

Pre-play events: List below the details, including effectively handling potential obstacles and a positive outcome. Then, visualize the event.

____

____

____

Shift to Positive Interpretations: Pause and challenge negative interpretations about yourself, situations and others.

Alternative Possibilities: ____

____

Productive Actions: ____

____

Give and Serve: Ways I can add value and focus on others. ________________

____

Have FUN!: What can I do just for fun, to recharge.

____

mPWR¹⁰ tool   Date ______________________

Create Goal Momentum:

Goal (as if achieved): ____

Note progress: ____

Next steps: ____

Goal (as if achieved): ____

Note progress: ____

Next steps: ____

Focus on What's Good: Things I am grateful for and/or are going well. Consider and include small specific things as well as strengths used.

1 ____

2 ____

3 ____

4 ____

5 ____

Pre-play events: List below the details, including effectively handling potential obstacles and a positive outcome. Then, visualize the event.

____

____

____

Shift to Positive Interpretations: Pause and challenge negative interpretations about yourself, situations and others.

Alternative Possibilities: ____

____

Productive Actions: ____

____

Give and Serve: Ways I can add value and focus on others. ______________

____

Have FUN!: What can I do just for fun, to recharge.

____

mPWR¹⁰ tool   Date _______________

Create Goal Momentum:

Goal (as if achieved): ____

Note progress: ____

Next steps: ____

Goal (as if achieved): ____

Note progress: ____

Next steps: ____

Focus on What's Good: Things I am grateful for and/or are going well. Consider and include small specific things as well as strengths used.

1 ____

2 ____

3 ____

4 ____

5 ____

Pre-play events: List below the details, including effectively handling potential obstacles and a positive outcome. Then, visualize the event.

____

____

____

Shift to Positive Interpretations: Pause and challenge negative interpretations about yourself, situations and others.

Alternative Possibilities: ______________________________________

____

Productive Actions: ____

____

Give and Serve: Ways I can add value and focus on others. _____________

____

Have FUN!: What can I do just for fun, to recharge.

____

mPWR¹⁰ tool   Date ________________

Create Goal Momentum:

Goal (as if achieved): ____

Note progress: ____

Next steps: ____

Goal (as if achieved): ____

Note progress: ____

Next steps: ____

Focus on What's Good: Things I am grateful for and/or are going well. Consider and include small specific things as well as strengths used.

1 ____

2 ____

3 ____

4 ____

5 ____

Pre-play events: List below the details, including effectively handling potential obstacles and a positive outcome. Then, visualize the event.

____

____

____

Shift to Positive Interpretations: Pause and challenge negative interpretations about yourself, situations and others.

Alternative Possibilities: ____

____

Productive Actions: ____

____

Give and Serve: Ways I can add value and focus on others. ________________

____

Have FUN!: What can I do just for fun, to recharge.

____

mPWR¹⁰ tool   Date _________________

Create Goal Momentum:

Goal (as if achieved): ____

Note progress: ____

Next steps: ____

Goal (as if achieved): ____

Note progress: ____

Next steps: ____

Focus on What's Good: Things I am grateful for and/or are going well. Consider and include small specific things as well as strengths used.

1 ____

2 ____

3 ____

4 ____

5 ____

Pre-play events: List below the details, including effectively handling potential obstacles and a positive outcome. Then, visualize the event.

____

____

____

Shift to Positive Interpretations: Pause and challenge negative interpretations about yourself, situations and others.

Alternative Possibilities: ____

____

Productive Actions: ____

____

Give and Serve: Ways I can add value and focus on others. _____________

____

Have FUN!: What can I do just for fun, to recharge.

____

mPWR¹⁰ tool

Date _______________

Create Goal Momentum:

Goal (as if achieved): ____

Note progress: ____

Next steps: ____

Goal (as if achieved): ____

Note progress: ____

Next steps: ____

Focus on What's Good: Things I am grateful for and/or are going well. Consider and include small specific things as well as strengths used.

1 ____

2 ____

3 ____

4 ____

5 ____

Pre-play events: List below the details, including effectively handling potential obstacles and a positive outcome. Then, visualize the event.

____

____

____

Shift to Positive Interpretations: Pause and challenge negative interpretations about yourself, situations and others.

Alternative Possibilities: ____

____

Productive Actions: ____

____

Give and Serve: Ways I can add value and focus on others. _____________

____

Have FUN!: What can I do just for fun, to recharge.

____

mPWR¹⁰ tool   Date ________________

Create Goal Momentum:

Goal (as if achieved): ____

Note progress: ____

Next steps: ____

Goal (as if achieved): ____

Note progress: ____

Next steps: ____

Focus on What's Good: Things I am grateful for and/or are going well. Consider and include small specific things as well as strengths used.

1 ____

2 ____

3 ____

4 ____

5 ____

Pre-play events: List below the details, including effectively handling potential obstacles and a positive outcome. Then, visualize the event.

____

____

____

Shift to Positive Interpretations: Pause and challenge negative interpretations about yourself, situations and others.

Alternative Possibilities: ____

____

Productive Actions: ____

____

Give and Serve: Ways I can add value and focus on others. _______________

____

Have FUN!: What can I do just for fun, to recharge.

____

mPWR¹⁰ tool

Date ________________

Create Goal Momentum:

Goal (as if achieved): _______________________________________

Note progress: _______________________________________

Next steps: _______________________________________

Goal (as if achieved): _______________________________________

Note progress: _______________________________________

Next steps: _______________________________________

Focus on What's Good: Things I am grateful for and/or are going well. Consider and include small specific things as well as strengths used.

1 _______________________________________

2 _______________________________________

3 _______________________________________

4 _______________________________________

5 _______________________________________

Pre-play events: List below the details, including effectively handling potential obstacles and a positive outcome. Then, visualize the event.

____

____

____

Shift to Positive Interpretations: Pause and challenge negative interpretations about yourself, situations and others.

Alternative Possibilities: _______________________________________

____

Productive Actions: _______________________________________

____

Give and Serve: Ways I can add value and focus on others. ____________

____

Have FUN!: What can I do just for fun, to recharge.

____

mPWR¹⁰ tool　　　　　　　　Date ________________

Create Goal Momentum:

Goal (as if achieved): ____

Note progress: ____

Next steps: ____

Goal (as if achieved): ____

Note progress: ____

Next steps: ____

Focus on What's Good: Things I am grateful for and/or are going well. Consider and include small specific things as well as strengths used.

1 ____

2 ____

3 ____

4 ____

5 ____

Pre-play events: List below the details, including effectively handling potential obstacles and a positive outcome. Then, visualize the event.

____

____

____

Shift to Positive Interpretations: Pause and challenge negative interpretations about yourself, situations and others.

Alternative Possibilities: ____

____

Productive Actions: ____

____

Give and Serve: Ways I can add value and focus on others. _____________

____

Have FUN!: What can I do just for fun, to recharge.

____

mPWR¹⁰ tool

Date ________________

Create Goal Momentum:

Goal (as if achieved): ____

Note progress: ____

Next steps: ____

Goal (as if achieved): ____

Note progress: ____

Next steps: ____

Focus on What's Good: Things I am grateful for and/or are going well. Consider and include small specific things as well as strengths used.

1 ____

2 ____

3 ____

4 ____

5 ____

Pre-play events: List below the details, including effectively handling potential obstacles and a positive outcome. Then, visualize the event.

____

____

____

Shift to Positive Interpretations: Pause and challenge negative interpretations about yourself, situations and others.

Alternative Possibilities: ______________________________________

____

Productive Actions: ____

____

Give and Serve: Ways I can add value and focus on others. _____________

____

Have FUN!: What can I do just for fun, to recharge.

____

mPWR¹⁰ tool

Date ___________________

Create Goal Momentum:

Goal (as if achieved): ____

Note progress: ____

Next steps: ____

Goal (as if achieved): ____

Note progress: ____

Next steps: ____

Focus on What's Good: Things I am grateful for and/or are going well. Consider and include small specific things as well as strengths used.

1 ____

2 ____

3 ____

4 ____

5 ____

Pre-play events: List below the details, including effectively handling potential obstacles and a positive outcome. Then, visualize the event.

____

____

____

Shift to Positive Interpretations: Pause and challenge negative interpretations about yourself, situations and others.

Alternative Possibilities: ____

____

Productive Actions: ____

____

Give and Serve: Ways I can add value and focus on others. ___________

____

Have FUN!: What can I do just for fun, to recharge.

____

mPWR¹⁰ tool

Date ________________

Create Goal Momentum:

Goal (as if achieved): ____

Note progress: ____

Next steps: ____

Goal (as if achieved): ____

Note progress: ____

Next steps: ____

Focus on What's Good: Things I am grateful for and/or are going well. Consider and include small specific things as well as strengths used.

1 ____

2 ____

3 ____

4 ____

5 ____

Pre-play events: List below the details, including effectively handling potential obstacles and a positive outcome. Then, visualize the event.

____

____

____

Shift to Positive Interpretations: Pause and challenge negative interpretations about yourself, situations and others.

Alternative Possibilities: ____

____

Productive Actions: ____

____

Give and Serve: Ways I can add value and focus on others. ________________

____

Have FUN!: What can I do just for fun, to recharge.

____

mPWR¹⁰ tool

Date ________________

Create Goal Momentum:

Goal (as if achieved): ____

Note progress: ____

Next steps: ____

Goal (as if achieved): ____

Note progress: ____

Next steps: ____

Focus on What's Good: Things I am grateful for and/or are going well. Consider and include small specific things as well as strengths used.

1 ____

2 ____

3 ____

4 ____

5 ____

Pre-play events: List below the details, including effectively handling potential obstacles and a positive outcome. Then, visualize the event.

____

____

____

Shift to Positive Interpretations: Pause and challenge negative interpretations about yourself, situations and others.

Alternative Possibilities: _______________________________________

____

Productive Actions: ____

____

Give and Serve: Ways I can add value and focus on others. _______________

____

Have FUN!: What can I do just for fun, to recharge.

____

mPWR¹⁰ tool

Date ___________________

Create Goal Momentum:

Goal (as if achieved): ____

Note progress: ____

Next steps: ____

Goal (as if achieved): ____

Note progress: ____

Next steps: ____

Focus on What's Good: Things I am grateful for and/or are going well. Consider and include small specific things as well as strengths used.

1 ____

2 ____

3 ____

4 ____

5 ____

Pre-play events: List below the details, including effectively handling potential obstacles and a positive outcome. Then, visualize the event.

____

____

____

Shift to Positive Interpretations: Pause and challenge negative interpretations about yourself, situations and others.

Alternative Possibilities: ____

____

Productive Actions: ____

____

Give and Serve: Ways I can add value and focus on others. ________________

____

Have FUN!: What can I do just for fun, to recharge.

____

mPWR¹⁰ tool   Date _________________

Create Goal Momentum:

Goal (as if achieved): ____

Note progress: ____

Next steps: ____

Goal (as if achieved): ____

Note progress: ____

Next steps: ____

Focus on What's Good: Things I am grateful for and/or are going well. Consider and include small specific things as well as strengths used.

1 ____

2 ____

3 ____

4 ____

5 ____

Pre-play events: List below the details, including effectively handling potential obstacles and a positive outcome. Then, visualize the event.

____

____

____

Shift to Positive Interpretations: Pause and challenge negative interpretations about yourself, situations and others.

Alternative Possibilities: _____________________________________

____

Productive Actions: ____

____

Give and Serve: Ways I can add value and focus on others. ______________

____

Have FUN!: What can I do just for fun, to recharge.

____

mPWR¹⁰ tool

Date ________________

Create Goal Momentum:

Goal (as if achieved): ____

Note progress: ____

Next steps: ____

Goal (as if achieved): ____

Note progress: ____

Next steps: ____

Focus on What's Good: Things I am grateful for and/or are going well. Consider and include small specific things as well as strengths used.

1 ____
2 ____
3 ____
4 ____
5 ____

Pre-play events: List below the details, including effectively handling potential obstacles and a positive outcome. Then, visualize the event.

____

____

____

Shift to Positive Interpretations: Pause and challenge negative interpretations about yourself, situations and others.

Alternative Possibilities: ____

____

Productive Actions: ____

____

Give and Serve: Ways I can add value and focus on others. ___________________

____

Have FUN!: What can I do just for fun, to recharge.

____

mPWR¹⁰ tool

Date ________________

Create Goal Momentum:

Goal (as if achieved): ____

Note progress: ____

Next steps: ____

Goal (as if achieved): ____

Note progress: ____

Next steps: ____

Focus on What's Good: Things I am grateful for and/or are going well. Consider and include small specific things as well as strengths used.

1 ____

2 ____

3 ____

4 ____

5 ____

Pre-play events: List below the details, including effectively handling potential obstacles and a positive outcome. Then, visualize the event.

____

____

____

Shift to Positive Interpretations: Pause and challenge negative interpretations about yourself, situations and others.

Alternative Possibilities: ____

____

Productive Actions: ____

____

Give and Serve: Ways I can add value and focus on others. ______________

____

Have FUN!: What can I do just for fun, to recharge.

____

mPWR¹⁰ tool

Date _______________

Create Goal Momentum:

Goal (as if achieved): _______________________________________

Note progress: _______________________________________

Next steps: _______________________________________

Goal (as if achieved): _______________________________________

Note progress: _______________________________________

Next steps: _______________________________________

Focus on What's Good: Things I am grateful for and/or are going well. Consider and include small specific things as well as strengths used.

1 _______________________________________

2 _______________________________________

3 _______________________________________

4 _______________________________________

5 _______________________________________

Pre-play events: List below the details, including effectively handling potential obstacles and a positive outcome. Then, visualize the event.

____

____

____

Shift to Positive Interpretations: Pause and challenge negative interpretations about yourself, situations and others.

Alternative Possibilities: _______________________________________

____

Productive Actions: _______________________________________

____

Give and Serve: Ways I can add value and focus on others. _______________

____

Have FUN!: What can I do just for fun, to recharge.

____

mPWR¹⁰ tool   Date ___________________

Create Goal Momentum:

Goal (as if achieved): ____

Note progress: ____

Next steps: ____

Goal (as if achieved): ____

Note progress: ____

Next steps: ____

Focus on What's Good: Things I am grateful for and/or are going well.
Consider and include small specific things as well as strengths used.

1 ____

2 ____

3 ____

4 ____

5 ____

Pre-play events: List below the details, including effectively handling potential
obstacles and a positive outcome. Then, visualize the event.

____

____

____

Shift to Positive Interpretations: Pause and challenge negative interpretations
about yourself, situations and others.

Alternative Possibilities: ____

____

Productive Actions: ____

____

Give and Serve: Ways I can add value and focus on others. ______________

____

Have FUN!: What can I do just for fun, to recharge.

____

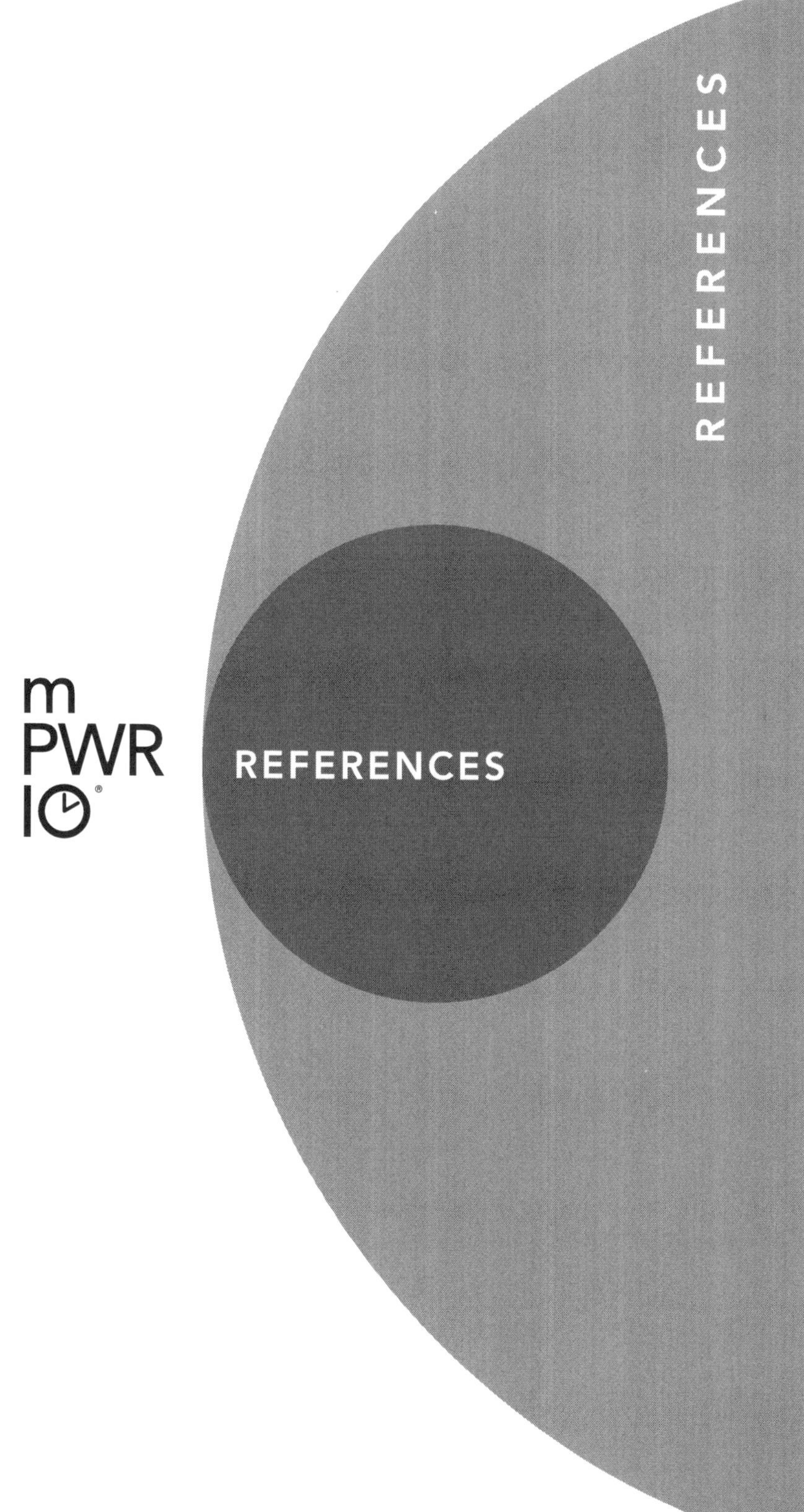
m
PWR
IO

REFERENCES

REFERENCES

mPWR10®

REFERENCES

References

Ben-Shahar, T. (2007). *Happier: Learn the Secrets to Daily Joy and Lasting Fulfillment.* (New York: McGraw-Hill), p. 71.

Blanchard, K. & Johnson, S. (1982). *The One Minute Manager.* (New York: Berkley Books), p. 39.

Danner, D. D., Snowdon, D. A., & Friesen, W. V. (2001). Positive emotions in early life and longevity: Findings from the Nun Study. *Journal of Personality and Social Psychology*, 80, 804-813.

Diener, E., Nickerson, C., Lucas, R., & Sandvik, E. (2000). Dispositional affect and job outcomes. *Social Indicators Research*, 59, 229-259.

Dowling, J. (2009). Personal communications.

Emmons, R. (2009) Highlights from the Research Project on Gratitude and Thankfulness *Dimensions and Perspectives of Gratitude*, http://psychology.ucdavis.edu/labs/emmons/, retrieved July 13 2009

Emmons, R. A. & McCullough, M. E. (2003). Counting Blessings Versus Burdens: An Experimental Investigation of Gratitude and Subjective Well-Being in Daily Life. *Journal of Personality and Social Psychology*, 84, 377-389.

Feltz, D. L., & Landers, D. M. (1983). The effects of mental practice on motor skills learning and performance: a meta analysis. *Journal of Sports Psychology*, 5, 25-57.

Fredrickson, B. L., & Joiner, T. (2002). Positive emotions trigger upward spirals toward emotional well-being. *Psychological Science*, 13, 172-175.

Fredrickson, B. L., Tugade, M. M., Waugh, C. E., & Larkin, G. (2003). What good are positive emotions in crisis? A prospective study of resilience and emotions following the terrorist attacks on the United States on September 11, 2001. *Journal of Personality and Social Psychology*, 84, 365-376.

Fredrickson, B. L., & Losada, M. (2005). Positive Affect and the Complex Dynamics of Human Flourishing. *American Psychologist*, 60, 678-686.

Hsieh, T. (2010). *Delivering Happiness, A Path To Profits, Passion, and Purpose.* (New York: Hachette Book Group), p. 45.

Izzo, J. (2008). *The Five Secrets You Must Discover Before You Die.* (San Francisco: Berrett-Koehler Publishers, Inc.), p. 126.

Jackson, H. (2010). Personal communications.

Knäuper, B., et al. (2011). Fruitful plans: Adding targeted mental imagery to implementation intentions increases fruit consumption. Psychology & Health, Feb 18: 1-17

Losada, M. (1999). The complex dynamics of high performance teams. *Mathematical and Computer Modelling*, 30 (9-10), 179-192.

Losada, M., & Heaphy, E. (2004). The Role of Positivity and Connectivity in the Performance of Business Teams. American Behavioral Scientist, 47, 740-765.

Lyubomirsky, S. (2008). *The How of Happiness: A New Approach to Getting the Life You Want.* (New York: Penguin Press), p. 20-21.

Lyubomirsky, S., King, L., & Diener, E (2005). The benefits of frequent positive affect: Does happiness lead to success? *Psychological Bulletin*, 131, 803-855.

Martin, K. A, & Hall, C. R (1995). Using mental imagery to enhance intrinsic motivation. *Journal of Sports & Exercise Psychology*, 17, 54-69.

Matthews, G. (2007): Study Backs up Strategies for Achieving Goals. http://www.dominican.edu/dominicannews/study-backs-up-strategies-for-achieving-goals.html, Retrieved February 24, 2011

Ostir, G. V., Markides, K. S., Black, S. A., & Goodwin J. S. (2000). Emotional well-being predicts subsequent functional independence and survival. *Journal of the American Geriatrics Society*, 48, 473-478.

Otake, K., et al. (2006). Happy People Become Happier Through Kindness: A Counting Kindnesses Intervention. *Journal of Happiness Studies*, 7, 361-375.

Seligman, M. (1990). *Learned Optimism: How to Change Your Mind and Your Life*. (New York: Pocket Books), p. 234.

Seligman, M. E. & Schulman, P. (1986). Explanatory Style as a Predictor of Productivity and Quitting Among Life Insurance Sales Agents. *Journal of Personality and Social Psychology*, 50, 832-838.

Staw, B. M., Sutton, R. I., & Pelled, L. H. (1994). Employee Positive Emotion and Favorable Outcomes at the Workplace. *Organization Science*, 5, 51-71.

Taylor, S. E., Pham, L. B., Rivkin, I. D., & Armor, D. A. (1998), Harnessing the Imagination: Mental Simulation, Self-Regulation, and Coping. *American Psychologist*, 53, 429-439.

Tracy, B. (1993). *Maximum Achievement: Strategies and Skills That Will Unlock Your Hidden Powers to Succeed*. (New York: Simon & Schuster Paperbacks), p. 98.

Williamson, M. (2006). *The Gift of Change: Spiritual Guidance for Living Your Best Life*. (New York: HarperCollins Publishers, Inc), p. 55, 117.

Woolfolk, R. L., Parrish, M. W., & Murphy, S. M. (1985). The effects of positive and negative imagery on motor skill performance. *Cognitive Therapy and Research*, 9, 335-341

Bring *On Track* to your organization, sales or athletic team

If you are interested in training sessions, keynotes, mobile web learning and/ or individual coaching based on the *On Track* principles, please contact *mPWR*[10] Partners at:

Online: www.mpwr10.com

Email: info@mpwr10.com

Michelle Chung: mchung@mpwr10.com

Nancy Donahue: ndonahue@mpwr10.com

 Facebook.com/mpwr10

 @mpwr10

About the authors:

Michelle Chung and Nancy Donahue met while working together in leadership positions at a large global pharmaceutical company. During this time in their professional careers they honed the skill of translating complex scientific information into approaches that physicians and patients could easily understand and apply to achieve optimal benefit. They also discovered a shared passion for helping people grow and thrive in their personal and professional lives. With this foundation, they were inspired to research, develop and field-test the *mPWR[10]* personal effectiveness program that uniquely enables people to take action and integrate proven habits essential for success. They deliver *mPWR[10]* training nationwide to fortune 500 companies, colleges, leaders, entrepreneurs, and individuals.

Michelle Chung

Michelle brings 18 years of progressive experience in the pharmaceutical industry encompassing marketing, lifecycle development, new product planning and sales leadership. Serving in senior leadership roles, she has developed and led many individuals and cross functional teams in both the United States and United Kingdom. Michelle's achievements include management of five successful marketing launches, leading brands with annual revenues of more than $500 million, and award winning sales leadership. Michelle can be reached at mchung@mpwr10.com.

Nancy Donahue

Nancy's experience spans 20 years of pharmaceutical sales, market development, marketing and executive management. As a member of the Executive Team, and serving as Senior Vice President of Sales and Marketing, Nancy built and led the commercial organization at Anesiva. During her 15 year tenure at GlaxoSmithKline, Nancy was Marketing Director of the diabetes franchise, launched, and led the team responsible for growing Coreg into a billion-dollar brand. Nancy can be reached at ndonahue@mpwr10.com.

Expert Contributor

Joseph Dowling, M.S., LPC has been a specialist in Peak-Performance Psychology for over 20 years and maintains a private practice in Philadelphia. In his work with corporate professionals and athletes, Joe utilizes a unique solution-focused, strength-based model and teaches a novel approach to easily and routinely access your peak-performance zone. He has authored numerous articles, has been an invited speaker at national Psychology conferences and guest lecturer at several universities.

www.mpwr10.com